THE ANTI-TERROR CHECKLIST

Bill Stanton

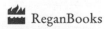
ReganBooks

HarperTorch

An Imprint of HarperCollins*Publishers*

HARPERTORCH
An Imprint of HarperCollins*Publishers*
10 East 53rd Street
New York, New York 10022-5299

Copyright © 2001 by William Stanton
ISBN: 0-06-009529-6

First HarperTorch paperback printing: October 2001

HarperCollins ®, HarperTorch™, and ❦ ™ are trademarks of HarperCollins Publishers Inc.

Printed in the United States of America

Visit HarperTorch on the World Wide Web at www.harpercollins.com
Visit ReganBooks on the World Wide Web at www.reganbooks.com

10 9 8 7 6 5 4 3 2 1

ATTENTION: ORGANIZATIONS AND CORPORATIONS
Most HarperTorch paperbacks are available at special quantity discounts for bulk purchases for sales promotions, premiums, or fund-raising. For information, please call or write:
Special Markets Department, HarperCollins Publishers, Inc., 10 East 53rd Street, New York, New York 10022-5299. Telephone: (212) 207-7528. Fax: (212) 207-7222.

THE
ANTI-TERROR
CHECKLIST

In memory of the best men I've ever known:
Jack Maple, Frankie Parlato,
and Grandpa Bill

INTRODUCTION

It is a fact of life: The world has changed. The terrorist attacks on the morning of September 11 on the World Trade Center and the Pentagon instantly and irrevocably altered our attitudes, our outlook, the very way we live. All of us know people who now, out of fear, are willing to deprive themselves of some of life's pleasures: they won't get on an airplane, or go into the city for dinner, or go to a crowded public place like a ball park, a concert, or even a mall or a movie.

Living in fear is no way to live.

How did this happen? Think of the United States as our house. Well, we the people—the residents of that house—have gone to bed with the windows wide open, the doors unlocked, and all our valuables laid out on the kitchen table. Translation: it was an invitation to disaster. Many people in the intelligence and security community, including me, had been quietly saying for quite some time that it was not a matter of *if*, but *when* serious terrorism would hit our shores. That time has obviously arrived. The government will now do its job to protect us as American citizens. But you shouldn't be satisfied to leave it at that. There are things we can do as individuals to help protect ourselves, our families, and our friends, just as we wear seat belts in the car and have smoke detectors in our homes.

We are now being tested in a way we haven't been tested before. How do we handle this unspeakable evil? When do we react? What should we do? Why should we do it? This is not a book about paranoia. It's a book about being prepared, being prudent, and taking precautions. The best way to handle any situation, of course, is to be prepared—especially in an emergency.

In nearly two decades as a New York City cop, a security consultant, and a private investigator, I have found that in a crisis the way people respond generally falls into one of five categories. There is the deer in the headlights, the person who is essentially immobilized by fear and does nothing. There's the ostrich, who simply denies that anything at all is wrong and, like the deer, does nothing. We also have the sheep, who just follows along with everyone else, even if it's the wrong thing to do. There's the chicken without a head, the frenzied person who runs around with boundless energy but without a clue about what to do. And finally there's the lion, the strong, composed person who takes charge and meets the challenge head on.

This book will help you become a lion. By educating yourself—doing your homework and learning what to do in an emergency—you'll help not only yourself, but those around you as well. Think of it in the same way you'd think of learning CPR. You may never actually need to use it, but if there were a situation even once in your life when you did, there's simply no way to put a price on having that knowledge.

I learned nearly twenty years ago when I was a cop in the South Bronx that the most effective weapon I had was not my gun or my canister of pepper spray or my nightstick. It was my mind. It was my common sense. Pat Rogers, a friend and colleague of mine in law enforcement and intelligence, says that without the proper mindset you're nowhere. "In major disasters like a cruise ship fire or a bus crash or a shooting," says Rogers, a retired marine and former counterterrorist operative, "you always see survivors being interviewed, and they all say exactly the same thing: 'I couldn't believe it was happening to me.' We call that Condition White." Condition White means that you're virtually unconscious, if not actually so. You never see it coming and have no idea how to react when something happens. "Condition Yellow," Rogers says, "is equivalent to the state you're in when driving a car. It's a sort of relaxed alertness. Condition Orange is when you are specifically alert to something—a guy following you on the street or some other suspicious activity. And Condition Red is when the stuff hits the fan, when the fight is on."

The goal of this book is to get you to elevate your normal, everyday frame of mind to Condition Yellow, that state of relaxed alertness—and to prepare you just in case you ever need to ratchet it up to Condition Orange, or perhaps even Condition Red. I don't want you to overreact. I just want you to recognize and understand that the best defense is to live our lives the way we want to, but at the same time, make the right preparations and take the proper precautions. It is the way people in other countries, in Israel, for example, have had to live for years.

My partner in the investigations business was a man named Jack Maple. Jack, who, sadly, died in summer 2001, was the best cop I ever knew. As deputy police commissioner of the New York Police Department, he dramatically reformed the department and cut crime in New York by unprecedented levels. His strategy, which is now used by police departments all over the world, was amazingly simple. He always used to say that you need accurate, timely intelligence; effective tactics; and relentless follow-up and assessment.

In other words, identify the problem, come up with a plan, and stay on top of things to make sure your plan is working. All of which is what I hope you'll do with this book. Read it, follow through on the exercises, write all over it, talk about it with your family and friends, and follow up periodically to make sure everyone's still prepared.

As John Steinbeck wrote, "The sword is more important than the shield, and skill is more important than either. The final weapon is the brain—all else is supplemental."

Bill Stanton
New York City
October 2001

TYPES OF THREAT

EXPLOSIVES

One thing distinguishes an explosive event from other kinds of terrorist attacks: brevity. Biological, chemical, and nuclear weapons have lasting effects that must be dealt with over a period of days and weeks, if not months. An explosion, on the other hand, is immediate—there's no fallout, no risk of contamination, and, as long as you're not at or near ground zero, no need to evacuate. Of course, explosive devices wreak their own special havoc. The attacks on the World Trade Center in New York and on the Pentagon demonstrated the kind of destructive power an explosive device, in this case a jetliner fully loaded with twenty thousand pounds of fuel, can have. Used strategically, it can even bring down a tower more than one hundred stories tall. More than five thousand people lost their lives on the morning of September 11—some from the initial impact of the plane, but many more when the structures began to deform and the buildings collapsed onto themselves.

There are a lot of ways of using many different kinds of materials to make a bomb, and in our high-tech world, explosive devices are a low-tech weapon. Simplicity and availability of ingredients are the reasons explosives remain the favorite means of attack for terrorists. "There'll be more attacks now and over the next five to eight years, and the bulk of them will be with guns and explosives," says retired marine Pat Rogers. "Perhaps at some later point the terrorists will move to weapons of mass destruction, but they are much harder to get." The World Trade Center attack was extraordinary both for the method used (planes as guided missiles) and the enormity of the destruction. More often than not, however, destruction is achieved by much less elaborate means, the most striking example being the 1995 attack on the Alfred P. Murrah Federal Office Building in Oklahoma City. In that case, common fertilizer was mixed with fuel to create a bomb that had the same effect as two thousand pounds of dynamite. Ammonium nitrate fertilizer can be bought for pennies at supply stores across the country; farmers have been using it in their fields for years. But when ammonium nitrate is mixed with a combustible agent, it becomes a powerful explosive. Blends of ammonium nitrate and fuel oil (referred to as ANFO) are available to construction crews and demolition companies, but their sale is closely watched by the government. Fortunately, it is very difficult (but certainly not impossible) to make the same blends at home.

What is of greater importance is not so much how something is being attacked (an explosion, after all, is an explosion), but what is being attacked. The two examples above show that common targets are large, enclosed facilities that usually have large numbers of people in them. The greater danger is when the target becomes its own agent of destruction. One only has to look back to the disastrous accidents in Chernobyl and Bhopal, India, to see what horrifying results occur when a major nuclear or chemical facility is compromised. In the case of Chernobyl, thirty-two people died within forty-eight hours, but radiation-related illnesses and deformities, some of which have resulted in death, still continue to this day and have affected the lives of tens of thousands (final death toll estimates run as high as thirty thousand). In Bhopal, a Union Carbide plant that manufactured pesticides malfunctioned and

leaked poisonous gas th
twenty-five hundred people
spread throughout the city.

Since the goal of terrorism is as
demoralize and destabilize a society as it is to destroy specific pieces of real estate, one must also be aware of secondary devices that explode after the initial blast. "Terrorists pick particular targets for two reasons," says Jerry Hauer, former director of New York's Office of Emergency Management and one of the world's leading experts on terrorism. "First, because they are symbols of America, like the World Trade Center and the Pentagon. And second, to cause disruption and fear. To get inside the heads of Americans and disturb their normal routines. And few acts get inside people's heads and are as demoralizing as that second explosion timed to kill emergency workers who respond to an attack." In the early 1980s, for example, the

IRA began planting two bombs at a single location, one set to explode a short while after the first one. The first bomb would do its own damage and create a panic. The second bomb might be set to go off a half an hour later, just as rescue teams arrived on the scene.

CHEMICAL WEAPONS

First off, let's clear some things up here. Chemical agents and biological agents are different. The popular media often confuse the two, leading many people to think that substances such as anthrax and Sarin are of the same family. They are not. For the purposes of this section, let's focus on chemical weapons and what their properties are in relation to their biological counterparts. "Biological weapons are those that involve the use of an organism to cause disease in the human population," notes Dr. Monica Schoch-Spana, senior fellow at the Johns Hopkins Center for Civilian Biodefense Studies. "They include viruses, bacteria, and bacterial toxins. Chemical weapons are synthetic substances with the capacity to cause casualties."

All chemical agents are artificially produced. None are found in nature. Chemical agents are produced only to be weapons— they have no use in industry, health care, or any other field of human endeavor. Chemical agents can be divided into several categories.

NERVE AGENTS

Known to scientists as organo-phosphorous compounds, nerve agents can be absorbed through the skin or by inhalation. Essentially, these agents disrupt the transmission of the electrical impulses that enable your nervous system to function properly. One common result of this is that muscles continue to contract when they shouldn't, and since breathing is a muscular activity, someone who has been exposed to a nerve agent begins to suffocate. Depending on the amount absorbed by the body, onset of symptoms can take as much as a half hour, or as little as a few minutes. Common nerve agents in military use include Sarin and VX. In 1995, a Japanese religious cult called the Aum Shinrikyo released Sarin—a colorless, odorless compound that inhibits the nervous system and can come in either a gas or a highly evaporative liquid— in the Tokyo subway system. Small packages of the liquid were placed on the floors of three trains that converged at a section of the city that is home to many government offices. The packages were surreptitiously placed on the floor of the trains by members of the cult, who then punctured them with umbrella points or simply kicked them around. Fortunately, the Sarin simply ran along the floor, evaporating slowly in the cold environment. As a result, only twelve people died instead of the hundreds or thousands that were intended. (It should be noted, however, that thousands were injured, suffering from convulsions, loss of consciousness, and difficulty breathing.) Later, in Aum Shinrikyo's offices, authorities found suitcase-like contraptions that contained vaporizers and fans. Such a device would have been far more deadly than the small packs of liquid used on the trains. As a liquid, Sarin remained fairly localized, but had it been distributed in gaseous form in a warmer environment, it would have spread far more quickly and effectively.

MUSTARD AGENT

Mustard agent (commonly referred to as mustard gas), a liquid or gas that causes chemical burns to the skin, irritation to the eyes, and difficulty breathing, was discovered in 1860. It was first used as a chemical weapon during World War I, and it was used (in a modernized, less odiferous form) as recently as in the mid-to-late 1980s by Iraq during its war with Iran. (It is projected that five hundred to one thousand Iranian soldiers died from mustard agent poisoning.)

Mustard agent is colorless and nearly odorless. Its name was derived from an earlier version that did in fact smell like mustard. Modern production of mustard agent yields something that some say smells like rotting onions, but it is a faint smell, and inhalation of mustard agent results in a dulling of the sense of smell anyway.

Mustard agent has been delivered in the past primarily through explosive shells fired from medium-sized artillery. A canister of mustard gas is inserted into the shell and released by a small explosive charge that detonates above its intended target. In theory, mustard agent could be vaporized and distributed from a low-flying plane (such as a crop duster) or slowly leaked from a pressurized tank in an enclosed environment. When absorbed into the human body (either through the skin or through inhalation), mustard agent begins to affect the skin, eyes, lungs, and gastrointestinal tract. Once in the bloodstream, mustard agent binds itself to the base compounds of an individual's DNA. The DNA molecule may then begin to break down, interfering with normal cellular activity. Blistering of the skin, akin to that of a burn victim, irritation and/or damage to the eyes, hoarseness, and difficulty breathing are common symptoms of mustard poisoning.

One especially troubling characteristic of mustard agent is its delayed effect. Someone exposed to it may not begin to develop symptoms for two to twenty-four hours after initial contact. Thereafter, the individual would experience discomfort breathing, irritated eyes, and skin irritation. By that point, the chemical has already begun its work damaging cells in those parts of the body, and it is much more difficult to treat than immediately after exposure.

HYDROGEN CYANIDE

This is a highly volatile liquid that hasn't been used very often, but was deployed during the Iran–Iraq war and again by Saddam Hussein against the Kurds in northern Iraq in the late 1980s. In 1982, seven people in the Chicago area died after ingesting Extra-Strength Tylenol capsules that had been laced with potassium cyanide. Each poisoned capsule contained thirty-five milligrams of the deadly compound. A lethal dose would have been five to seven micrograms, meaning that the pills had up to ten thousand times the necessary amount to kill someone. In one of the great product recalls of all time, parent company Johnson & Johnson recalled thirty-one million bottles of Tylenol and went on a national media blitz to warn consumers not to take any Tylenol product until the matter was resolved. The Tylenol Killer, as the perpetrator has come to be known, was never caught. Zyklon B, the gas used at Nazi death camps, is also a form of hydrogen cyanide.

Many forms of cyanide, including those mentioned, are readily available in various industries: cyanide salts are used in the electroplating of metals, and cyanide is used in developing X-ray film and to fumigate ships and warehouses (properly handled, it will kill vermin and insects that may reside within). Cyanide is so toxic because of the way it acts upon metal-containing enzymes at the cellular level. Like most of the substances discussed here, cyanide binds with the important enzyme cytochromoxidase, which contains iron. By binding with the enzyme, cyanide renders it inoperable. Cytochromoxidase is responsible for such basic functions as cell respiration, and if a cell cannot breathe it will die. Cyanide is so powerful that it can have this effect on the majority of cells in the body within a very short time.

Cyanide exists in both liquid and gaseous form. It could contaminate a water supply, though it would have to be close to the point of ingestion. Poisoning a reservoir would, according to a United Nations study, require far too great an amount—about ten tons of potassium cyanide—to make it a real concern. Poisoning an office building's plumbing system, or even a local water-treatment plant, would be much easier. In addition, cyanide can be released as a gas, though its high volatility makes it poorly suited to outdoor environments. It doesn't take a lot of cyanide to kill someone. As mentioned, only five to seven micrograms are required. However, if the body is exposed to a smaller amount, treatable symptoms include loss of consciousness, nausea, and convulsions.

In spite of their use in military applications, chemical weapons would be difficult for a terrorist to employ successfully. They are simply not practical; while many of their constituent ingredients are available via commercial and industrial outlets, they are only effective when used in large quantities. Large amounts of dangerous and volatile chemicals are difficult to conceal and even harder to transport. The handling and preparation of these chemicals also poses a risk to the terrorists themselves. This may not seem like a problem for someone willing to kill himself for a cause, but this danger does raise the possibility of death before an attack could be carried out.

BIOLOGICAL WEAPONS

Of all the methods a terrorist could use to wage an attack on large numbers of people, biological agents generate the most fear and fascination—and for good reason. Explosive devices are highly localized and immediate. Chemical agents work within a localized area and within a reasonably short period of time. Biological weapons, on the other hand, can spread initially undetected throughout a large population, and in some cases, quite quickly. Their symptoms can take days, even weeks, to appear, so there is no unified event that draws the attention of the medical community. To put it another way, if there's an explosion at an office building, it's immediately apparent that firefighters and rescue workers should be called to the scene. Even chemical weapons have a comparatively short incubation period and, furthermore, are not contagious. But biological weapons lay low for a while, and even when they do appear, come across as something far more benign. "What people need to understand is that each pathogen produces its own disease process," notes Dr. Monica Schoch-Spana of Johns Hopkins. "You may not have symptoms for weeks. The length of it depends on the pathogen. Unfortunately, many of the agents present vague, flu-like symptoms."

The medical community is, sad to say, woefully unprepared to put the pieces together. How could it be any different? After the attacks on the World Trade Center and the Pentagon, the cities of New York and Washington D.C. put all local hospitals on alert to watch out for anything unusual, in fear of a biological agent. But how long could that monitoring continue? And what about every other locality in the United States? The great fear about biological weapons is that they can be introduced into a population without incident, and not until long after the perpetrators have left the country will their effects be known.

Dr. Schoch-Spana feels that the health care industry needs to be constantly aware. "What will be most helpful in determining if a biological weapon has been used is vigilant clinicians who report atypical patterns to the health department," she says. "If the health department gets word of it, they can look at it from a bird's-eye view. People should notice if patients in the prime of life start showing up with symptoms that are out of season for the usual causes. There's a seasonality to illness, and if something doesn't fit the templates, you get a gut feeling. If you call the health department, they can send out an epidemiologist to investigate."

It is currently believed that seventeen countries (including the United States, North Korea, Iraq, and Russia) are in possession of some sort of biological arsenal. Unfortunately, some of those nations are less than stable, and it is feared that such technology could wind up in the wrong hands for the right price. Prior to its Sarin attack on the Tokyo subway, the Aum Shinrikyo cult had made nine separate attempts to release anthrax and botulism into various parts of the capital city. All were unsuccessful. While botulism is considered to be a lesser threat (it is very treatable and not contagious), the use of anthrax by terrorist groups has long been a subject of concern. Anthrax and smallpox pose the greatest threat to health and public safety.

ANTHRAX

Anthrax comes in two forms. It is found in nature as a soil-based bacteria; in this form it may be introduced into the bloodstream by eating contaminated meat or by coming into contact with an open wound, say, while gardening. This form of anthrax is highly treatable with antibiotics.

The kind of anthrax that keeps everyone up at night is what is known as inhalational anthrax. Microscopic spores are created from the bacteria and can fly through the air. By going through the lungs, the bacteria can be absorbed more fully and quickly into the bloodstream. Once that happens, the bacteria spores begin to grow, and sufferers show up at their doctor's office saying they "just don't feel so well." The problem is that these mild symptoms develop slowly and then can take weeks to become more serious, and all the while the spores are still growing at a rate that makes treatment difficult, if not impossible. Ultimately, the toxins released by the bacteria will kill the host, which happens to approximately 90 percent of all people who have contracted this form of anthrax.

Fortunately, anthrax is not contagious, and the spores are somewhat fragile in that they are susceptible to a number of environmental concerns (for example, they can't survive long in direct sunlight). There is a vaccine, but its distribution has been limited to military personnel. Since the terrorist attacks on September 11, there has been talk of developing a vaccine for civilian use. In October 2001, three Floridians who all worked at the American Media company headquarters in Boca Raton were diagnosed with anthrax. It was suspected that the spores arrived with the mail and were inadvertently released into the building. One man died. Officials proceeded with a criminal investigation, but the isolated nature of the incident led most to believe it was unrelated to any form of widespread bioterrorism. Adding to public concern and fear was another isolated anthrax diagnosis in New York City, which was not fatal, but this was also thought to be unrelated to bioterrorism.

Only eighteen cases of pulmonary anthrax were reported in this country in the last century. As recently as 2000, a farmer was diagnosed with cutaneous anthrax (anthrax that had been contracted through the skin). He had disposed of five cows on his farm, one of which had the bacteria. Despite having worn leather gloves during their disposal, he found a small lesion on his cheek four days after he had handled the cows. He went to see his physician and was placed on a regimen of Ciprofloxacin, an antibiotic that is successful in treating anthrax. In a few weeks, he had fully recovered. Again, because anthrax bacteria are found in nature, the disease will occasionally infect people, particularly those who work in farming and agriculture. Not every case is reason to think that a terrorist act is taking place.

SMALLPOX

Smallpox may be the most frightening of all the potential biological threats. When it existed as a naturally occurring disease, smallpox was responsible for the deaths of untold millions of people. Although the disease has been known for more than three thousand years, its greatest terror has been known in comparatively modern times. At its height in the seventeenth and eighteenth centuries, smallpox killed 10 percent of the

European population, but its mortality rate skyrocketed to 90 percent when it first arrived in the New World. In fact, the entire population of the island of Hispaniola in the Caribbean, two and a half million native people, died from smallpox that was introduction by the Spanish settlers. By the twentieth century, eradication efforts were under way by means of a vaccine, and by 1980 the World Health Organization declared that smallpox had been eradicated across the globe.

What makes smallpox particularly dangerous is its high level of communicability. It can be passed from person to person simply by breathing the same air. Its long incubation period means that people will start complaining about symptoms as much as two weeks after they have been exposed, and even then the symptoms will be vague and seemingly not serious. Health care institutions may not be prepared to identify the disease—and may fail to isolate infected patients, leaving them free to spread the virus.

The United States stopped vaccinating children against smallpox in 1972. If you were born before 1972, you were vaccinated, but you're not in the clear—smallpox vaccines only last about ten years. But if smallpox was eradicated by a global vaccination effort almost twenty years ago, why should you be concerned? Well, two locations in the world are known to have preserved strains of the virus: the Centers for Disease Control in Atlanta, Georgia, and Vector, the Russian government's bioweapon storage facility in Koltsovo, Russia. While the Atlanta facility is considered secure, one cannot be as sanguine about the facility in the former Soviet Union.

When the virus enters the body, it attaches itself to interior membranes of the nose as well as to the mucous linings of the lungs. Then it migrates to the lymph nodes, spleen, and bone marrow. By this point the virus is circulating freely throughout the bloodstream, and it settles in areas beneath the skin and around the mouth and throat. Sufferers initially complain of fever, headaches, and back pain. Ultimately, victims will develop thousands of pustules that cover the body from head to toe. One third of all sufferers will die, including any that suffer hemorrhagic smallpox, which attacks immunocompromised individuals and destroys the connective tissue of the internal organs.

Fortunately, we do have the tools to inoculate our population against smallpox, as we did up until 1972, but only fifteen million doses of vaccine currently exist in the United States. The Centers for Disease Control have placed an order for another forty million, but they are not expected for another two years.

BOTULISM

Botulism is an illness brought about by ingesting the nerve-damaging toxin produced by the anaerobic bacterium *clostridium botulinum*. Adults can contract the toxin through a wound or through eating contaminated foods. Infants are able to create the toxin themselves if they eat the bacteria, making them even more susceptible to illness. The type of botulism poisoning that warrants the most attention is food-borne. The bacteria grow best in low-oxygen environments, so canned goods are potential carriers, particularly if they were canned by hand. Unrefrigerated meats may also be a breeding ground for the bacteria.

Like a nerve agent, botulism attacks the synapse of nerves, prohibiting the release of the neurotransmitter acetylcholine, which then results in paralysis, most notably respiratory paralysis. The bacteria cannot penetrate intact skin but can enter through a wound or, more commonly, through eating contaminated food. People who are properly diagnosed and treated may require a respirator.

Botulism can be distributed either in aerosol form or by contaminating food products. Though they did not use botulism, a cult in Oregon called the Rajaneeshees attempted in 1984 to contaminate the food at a number of local stores by spraying it with salmonella. Salmonella is a bacterium that enters the bloodstream when you eat infected foods (particularly undercooked chicken and eggs, but the bacteria can also appear in peanut butter, chocolate, and milk) and inflames the small intestine. While no one died, seven hundred fifty people suffered acute gastrointestinal problems. If botulism had been distributed this way, many people would have died.

The largest botulism outbreak in recent history occurred in 1977 in Pontiac, Michigan, when a cook at a local restaurant served customers some home-canned jalapeño peppers that had been incorrectly sealed. Fifty-nine people became ill. There were no fatalities because the botulism anti-toxin supply maintained by the CDC is very effective; in the past fifty years the fatality rate among people exposed to botulism has gone from 50 percent to 8 percent—and botulism is not contagious, making it relatively easy to control.

TULAREMIA

Tularemia is a bacterium that can cause plague-like (but less severe) effects in humans. It was first discovered in humans in the United States in 1914. Found in animals like rabbits, water rats, and squirrels, tularemia was looked at by both the Japanese and American governments in World War II as a potential biological weapon. The United States and the Soviet Union stockpiled tularemia for several years during the cold war, with the United States destroying its supply in 1973 and the Soviet Union getting rid of its stock in the early 1990s. According to the American Medical Association, distribution of tularemia via aerosol would be widely effective. The June 2001 *Journal of the American Medical Association* stated, "The Working Group on Civilian Biodefense considers F tularensis to be a dangerous potential biological weapon because of its extreme infectivity, ease of dissemination, and substantial capacity to cause illness and death."

In 1970 a World Health Organization panel determined that if fifty kilograms of tularemia were dropped over a city of five million people, there would be two hundred fifty thousand injuries, including nineteen thousand deaths. Tularemia is so virulent that simply looking at an open petri dish of it could infect you. The bacteria are so hardy that they can travel through the air under a multitude of conditions and enter your lungs quite easily. They will then attack the spleen, lymph nodes, lungs, liver, and kidneys. Thus far, tularemia has not been passed between humans. Glandular swelling is a common symptom of tularemia, as well as fever and other symptoms that resemble pneumonia. With current treatment standards, the mortality rate for tularemia is down to 2 percent, but its occurrence is fairly infrequent under normal circumstances.

NUCLEAR WEAPONS

The old cold war–era fear was a sky full of Soviet ICBMs raining down on our major cities and military installations. In the new world, fear of nuclear weapons is far narrower in scope, but equally terrifying. The threat now is not three hundred missiles, or even thirty, but just one—perhaps loaded onto the back of a truck or shoved into a suitcase. The potential for death and destruction from just one weapon, strategically used, is almost incalculable.

Fortunately, the technical expertise and materials required to fabricate a weapon of this kind are so rare and expensive that it seems unlikely that any group could do it on its own. On the other hand, it's not impossible to imagine a breakaway Soviet republic selling equipment or engineering talent to the highest bidder. And while no country would like to be on the receiving end of a United States nuclear retaliation, a rogue group might feel it has nothing to lose. Pat Rogers, a noted counter-terrorism expert, is reasonably concerned about that possibility. "Can you find the people out there who know how to make these?" he asks. "Yes. Can you get your hands on the proper equipment? Yes. Is it very hard to move this stuff around, and can we detect it? Yes."

The greater threat is what would happen if a nuclear facility were compromised. The Chernobyl accident of 1985 was the result of poorly trained staff operating with few safety regulations. Their lack of experience resulted in a catastrophic chain of events that resulted in a large fireball blasting through the containment structure of one of the reactors, which allowed a cloud of radioactive particles to be admitted into the atmosphere. The neighboring town of Pryp'yat (population: thirty thousand) had to be evacuated, and while only thirty-two people died initially, many more suffered radiation-related illnesses and died in the weeks and months that followed. Even to this day, thousands of people in the area have been more susceptible to both cancer and birth defects than people in other regions.

THE CHECKLISTS
HOW TO PREPARE
FOR AN EMERGENCY

CHECKLIST 1

ESTABLISH A NETWORK

This is the critical first step in any emergency plan. Before you do anything else, you must determine who is on your team. The list of members is up to you, but you should think about this carefully. Include only those people you feel you need and/or want to be responsible for you, and vice-versa—that is, people whose team you want to be on so that they will look out for you as well. At the very least, your team consists of your immediate family, but it could include extended family who live nearby, close friends, and coworkers. You must know who you'll be communicating with and who you're planning for. First, think: in addition to immediate family, what relatives, friends, and coworkers live near you? Then, on the pages that follow, write down the names and contact information for your team.

TEAM MEMBERS

Name _____

Address_____

Phone _____

Cell/car phone _____

Beeper/pager _____

E-mail _____

Name _____

Address_____

Phone _____

Cell/car phone _____

Beeper/pager _____

E-mail _____

Name _____

Address_____

Phone _____

Cell/car phone _____

Beeper/pager _____

E-mail _____

List additional team members on page 89.

CHECKLIST 2

DESIGNATE A TEAM LEADER

Choosing the right leader is always important, and never more so than in this situation. This is the person who will essentially guide you and the team through the crisis. The team leader will assess the threat, analyze the risks, and determine the course of action. This includes, of course, which pre-determined plan to implement. It's a good idea to pick an alternate as well, in case the team leader is incapable of establishing communication. Redundancy is important: remember, you're planning for an emergency. Designate the team leader, and make sure that person is willing and able to fulfill the requirements of the team leader as outlined in this list.

TEAM LEADER'S CHECKLIST

Assess the threat _____

_____

Analyze the risks _____

_____

_____

Determine the course of action _____

_____

_____

ALTERNATE LEADER'S CHECKLIST

Assess the threat _____

_____

Analyze the risks _____

_____

_____

Determine the course of action _____

_____

_____

CHECKLIST 3

PREPARE A DETAILED
CONTACT SHEET

Actually, this should be broken into three lists: primary, secondary, and tertiary. The primary list must have all the information you might need to contact the people in your network. This means all their phone numbers (office, home, car, and cell) as well as beepers, pagers, and e-mail addresses. In the case of children, be sure to include phone numbers for schools, camps, babysitters, and any other places they might be during the day. The list should also include their social security numbers and medical information, such as their allergies and any medications they take for diabetes, high blood pressure, epilepsy, or any other condition.

CONTACT LIST ONE

MY NETWORK

Name _____

Address_____

Home phone _____

Cell/car phone _____

Beeper/pager _____

E-mail _____

Social security number _____

Medical information _____

Name _____

Address_____

Home phone _____

Cell/car phone _____

Beeper/pager _____

E-mail _____

Social security number _____

Medical information _____

MY NETWORK

Name _____

Address _____

Home phone _____

Cell/car phone _____

Beeper/pager _____

E-mail _____

Social security number _____

Medical information _____

_____

Name _____

Address _____

Home phone _____

Cell/car phone _____

Beeper/pager _____

E-mail _____

Social security number _____

Medical information _____

_____

MY NETWORK

Name _____

Address_____

Home phone _____

Cell/car phone _____

Beeper/pager _____

E-mail _____

Social security number _____

Medical information _____

_____

Name _____

Address_____

Home phone _____

Cell/car phone _____

Beeper/pager _____

E-mail _____

Social security number _____

Medical information _____

_____

CONTACT LIST TWO

The secondary list should contain contact numbers for doctors—including general practitioners, pediatricians, cardiologists, psychiatrists, any medical professional you think will you need in case of an emergency—as well as pharmacies and hospitals in the immediate area and wherever your fallback location will be (more about this on page 66).

CONTACT LIST TWO

IN MY IMMEDIATE AREA

Doctors _____

_____

Pharmacies _____

_____

Hospitals_____

_____

Department of Health_____

_____

IN THE FALLBACK AREA

Doctors _____

_____

Pharmacies _____

_____

Hospitals_____

_____

Department of Health_____

_____

CONTACT LIST THREE

The tertiary list should have numbers for the local police station (in addition to 911), as well as hotline numbers for the Centers for Disease Control, transportation, traffic reports, car rental (near home and work), and a car service phone number.

CONTACT LIST THREE

Emergency service __911_____

Local police _____

State police _____

Poison control_____

Disease control_____

Traffic reports

    Phone number_____

    Radio frequency _____

Car rental agencies

    Near home _____

    _____

    Near work_____

    _____

Car service_____

CHECKLIST 4

ESTABLISH A COMMAND POST

Ideally, the command post should be the home of someone out of state, a person not likely to be affected by the same emergency. However, this person must be easily and quickly accessible and have a computer with an Internet connection and a multi-line phone or a phone with call waiting.

It's very important to choose the right person because he or she will be responsible for establishing and coordinating all communication for your network. Whoever is at the command post should be able to handle stress, juggle multiple tasks under pressure, and be Internet savvy. So think hard about whom to choose for the command post. Make sure that every person on the team, not just the leader, knows who this person is, since each member will be contacting the command post for coordination and guidance.

COMMAND POST CHECKLIST

TEAM MEMBERS

Name _____

Address _____

Phone _____

E-mail _____

Name _____

Address _____

Phone _____

E-mail _____

Name _____

Address _____

Phone _____

E-mail _____

Name _____

Address _____

Phone _____

E-mail _____

CHECKLIST 5

CHOOSE A RENDEZVOUS POINT

This is the place where everyone in your network will meet before continuing on to their fallback/safe haven location (if time permits). Choose a backup rendezvous point as well. The backup should be an adequate distance from the primary location and/or reachable by a different route or means so that if events prohibit access to your primary meeting point you'll still be able to get to your backup location.

RENDEZVOUS POINT CHECKLIST

PRIMARY

Location _____

Contact person_____

Phone _____

Directions_____

_____

_____

_____

BACKUP

Location _____

Contact person_____

Phone _____

Directions_____

_____

_____

_____

CHECKLIST 6

PICK A SAFE HAVEN

Your safe haven is the place that everyone on your team will try to get to in an emergency. As they say in the real estate business, location is everything. The safe haven should be outside the danger zone. But, since you can't know for certain where and how wide the danger zone will be until a crisis actually occurs, how can you choose a safe haven? Here's how. If you live and work in a major city, pick a central point. For example, in New York that point would be the Empire State building, which is more or less in the middle of the city. Now, pick a safe haven that is at least fifty miles away from that point in any direction. A country house or a relative's house would be perfect. If these are not realistic options, choose a hotel that meets the criteria.

SAFE HAVEN CHECKLIST

PRIMARY

Name _____

Phone _____

Distance _____

Directions_____

_____

_____

_____

BACKUP

Name _____

Phone _____

Distance _____

Directions_____

_____

_____

_____

CHECKLIST 7

LEARN THE GEOGRAPHY

All members of your network should have a
road atlas. In addition, everyone should have
clearly marked maps that detail three routes
to the first rendezvous point and/or your safe
haven (MapQuest and other Internet sites
are great sources for this). One map should
delineate the primary route (highways); another should show the secondary route (side
streets and back roads); and a third map
should detail the available public transportation routes.

GEOGRAPHY CHECKLIST

Make sure you have:

❏ Map with detailed route to the rendezvous point/safe haven via major highways

❏ Map with detailed route to the rendezvous point/safe haven via side streets or back roads if major highways are not accessible

❏ Map with detailed route to the rendezvous point/safe haven via public transportation if driving is not possible

CHECKLIST 8

DELEGATE AND ASSIGN
RESPONSIBILITIES

Each member of the team should have pre-determined responsibilities he or she will carry out when an emergency occurs. For example, decide the following:

Who will pick up the children from school, camp, or the babysitter?

Who will pick up the elderly or infirm?

Who will pick up the pets?

Who will pick up the emergency kit (see description on page 78)?

In the event of a chemical or biological threat, if you cannot leave the immediate area due to quarantine, who is responsible for securing your residence and creating a safe room (more about this on page 86)?

Who is the "floater," the person who can take on whatever unexpected tasks arise? (The floater should have his/her own transportation.)

ASSIGNMENT OF RESPONSIBILITIES

_____will pick up the children.

_____will contact and pick up
the elderly or infirm.

_____will pick up the pets.

_____will pick up and transport
the emergency kit.

_____will secure the home and
create a safe room.

_____ will be the floater.

CHECKLIST 9

MONEY

Each network member should establish a fund to ensure they have enough readily available cash in case of emergency. Credit cards are good to have, but bear in mind the possibility of disruption in credit card communication systems. There should be enough to cover at least four nights at a motel, plus food and ancillary expenses. Tailor the list on the facing page based on the average cost of such expenses in your area.

MONEY

$ _____ Cost of four nights at motel or hotel

$ _____ Cost of food for the number of people on the team

$ _____ Cash for gas for four days

Cash for ancillary expenses:

$ _____ Medicine

$ _____ Sundries

CHECKLIST 10

WHAT IF?

Everyone in your network should sit down together and go over some "what if" scenarios. For example:

What if members of the network cannot establish communication?
Wait a predetermined amount of time and then go into your contingency plan so that each member is able to operate independently. Remember, the goal is to reach your safe haven.

What if someone cannot fulfill his or her responsibility?
Each member of the team should have secondary responsibilities that will kick in if another member of the network is unable to carry out his or her assignment.

What if your primary means of transportation is not available?

Find another way to get to your destination—share a ride with someone, or check in with the command post to see if someone in your network can make a detour and pick you up.

What if members of your network cannot get out of the danger zone due to a lockdown by law enforcement?

Anyone left in the danger zone should try to establish a network within the network, with the command post improvising contingency plans for you. The members of the network outside the danger zone should continue to follow the existing plan.

IMPORTANT NOTE: This plan is only as effective as your ability to carry it out. Regular drills should be conducted at least three times a year to make sure everyone understands the plan and is clear on what to do. This also allows for updating.

CHECKLIST 11

THE EMERGENCY KIT

Part of being prepared to act in a crisis is having the things you'll need to help get you through. Put together an emergency kit and keep it stored in an easily accessible place. You can keep the items in a backpack or a carton or even a small trash can.

EMERGENCY KIT

GENERAL SUPPLIES

❏ Food (non-perishable and canned goods)
❏ Bottled water (one gallon per person per day, by the recommendation of the American Red Cross)
❏ Sleeping bags and/or blankets
❏ Flashlight
❏ Radio
❏ Batteries (including cell phone batteries)
❏ First aid kit (including any needed prescription medication)
❏ Light sticks
❏ Maps
❏ Cash
❏ Smoke hood
❏ Toiletries
❏ Manual can opener
❏ Portable heater
❏ Copy of this book

CAR SUPPLIES

- ❏ Jumper cables
- ❏ Flat tire kit
- ❏ Spare tire
- ❏ Flares
- ❏ Flashlight
- ❏ Blanket
- ❏ Short rubber hose (for siphoning gas)
- ❏ First aid kit
- ❏ WD-40
- ❏ Cat litter (for traction in heavy snow)
- ❏ Bungee cords
- ❏ Tool kit

EXOTIC EQUIPMENT

Gas masks: These have suddenly become very popular, for obvious reasons. The problem with a gas mask, however, is that it's not going to be very effective unless you're willing to wear it all the time. By the time you're aware of the need to put it on, you've probably already been exposed to whatever contaminant has been released. Nevertheless, if you still feel that owning one might give you the upper hand in a disaster, it's important to keep a couple of things in mind. Don't pick up a used model at the local army-navy store. It could be old, damaged, or not up to current standards. Better to purchase such equipment from reputable haz-mat supply houses (the kind that sell to fire departments).

When buying a new gas mask, make sure it meets NATO specifications and is classified as an NBC mask. This means that the mask will filter out biological contaminants, chemical toxins, and nuclear radiated elements (e.g., radioactive dust particles). If you have children under the age of eight, you have to buy a child-size mask for them; adult-size gas masks don't work on children and can even be dangerous. Any good gas mask will also allow you to change the filter while your mask is on so that you will not be exposed to any danger.

Haz-mat suits: Full-body protection such as the kind worn by emergency workers will shield you from agents that can be absorbed through the skin. But they are large, unwieldy suits that cost between $600 and $1,600. Many require a SCBA (self-contained breathing apparatus) to work in conjunction with the suit. Some are aluminized to protect the wearer in case of fire. These kinds of suits are most effective when worn by someone who knows he's heading into a hazardous situation. However, when they're put on in response to an emergency already in progress, it's pretty much like closing the barn door after the horses have already gone. It's probably too late to provide any real protection.

Gas detectors: These can be broken down into two groups: those that can tell you specifically what substances are in the air, and those that can't identify particular substances but can alert you that something is wrong with the air's composition. The first kind can cost thousands of dollars and requires an air pump to take samples. It is intended for use by the military. The simplified version of the gas detector costs approximately $250 and can be held in the palm of your hand.

Antibiotics and vaccines:

- Smallpox has no treatment other than supportive therapy and antibiotics.

- The effect of nerve agents can be countered by a rapid injection of atropine into the leg. (United States military personnel carry a self-injector with them.)

- Anthrax will respond to antibiotics such as Cipro, but only before symptoms appear (after that, the disease has a 90 percent mortality rate). There is an anthrax vaccine, but its effectiveness has been questioned and it is only given to the military. It has also been found to have adverse side effects in many people, particularly children.

- Botulism can be treated with an anti-toxin, which is made available nationwide through the Centers for Disease Control.

- Tularemia has been successfully treated with such antibiotics as Streptomycin and Gentamicin, as well as Zithromax, Levoquin, and tetracyclines.

CHECKLIST 12

SECURING YOUR HOME

In the event of a quarantine or a lockdown by the government that forces you to remain in the danger zone, your home will become the safe haven, and all the supplies and criteria applied to the safe haven location in Checklist 6 go into effect for your secured home. It is also a good idea to do what many Israelis have done over the years: create a safe room inside your house.

THE HOME AS SAFE HAVEN

Close off and tape up:

- ❏ all air vents
- ❏ windows
- ❏ chimneys
- ❏ air conditioning vents
- ❏ door jams

Make sure you have:

- ❏ A HEPA air filter to run while the house is sealed.
- ❏ A portable generator in the basement.

FINAL CHECKLIST

1. Assess the threat.

2. Analyze the risks.

3. Establish communication with your network.

4. The team leader chooses the best option.

5. Coordinate tasks with your team via the command post.

6. Make any necessary adjustments to your plan.

7. Secure the transportation.

8. Pick up the children, elderly, infirm, and pets.

9. Proceed to your rendezvous point.

10. Head to your safe haven.

NOTES

ACKNOWLEDGMENTS

Thank you to the following people: John Miller, Bill Bratton, Jerry Hauer, Pat Rogers, Albert Sessa, Tom Fahey, Tom Fitzgerald, Dr. Jane Fitzgerald, Dr. Emilio Biagotti, Dr. Steve Pearlman, David Zinczenko, Frank DaConti, the late John O'Neil, Ricky Kilmer, Mike Swain, Kevin Berg, Johnny D., Michael Barrett, Delmar Coursey, Chief Louis Anamone, Lieutenant Al Parlato, Gunsite Ranch, Len Irish, Sam Grobart, Pam Pfeiffer, Cassie Jones, Lucy Albanese, Kris Tobiassen, Kellan Peck, Rhea Braunstein, Gregory Plonowski, Kurt Andrews, Cal Morgan, Paul Schnee, and Judith Regan.